New Design in WOOD

New Design in

WOOD

Donald J. Willcox

VNR VAN NOSTRAND REINHOLD COMPANY
NEW YORK CINCINNATI TORONTO LONDON MELBOURNE

OTHER BOOKS IN THIS SERIES:

NEW DESIGN IN CERAMICS

NEW DESIGN IN JEWELRY

NEW DESIGN IN STITCHERY

NEW DESIGN IN WEAVING

Van Nostrand Reinhold Company Regional Offices:
New York   Cincinnati   Chicago   Millbrae   Dallas

Van Nostrand Reinhold Company Foreign Offices:
London   Toronto   Melbourne

Designed by Myron Hall III
Printed by Halliday Lithograph Corporation
Color printed by Toppan Printing Company, Limited, Japan
Bound by Complete Books Company

Published by Van Nostrand Reinhold Company
450 West 33rd Street, New York, N.Y. 10001

Published simultaneously in Canada by
Van Nostrand Reinhold Ltd.

16   15   14   13   12   11   10   9   8   7   6   5   4   3   2   1

For
HHW and FCW
and for
FB and EB

CONTENTS

FOREWORD

For more than half a century Scandinavia has enjoyed a position of world leadership in the creation of wood forms of all types, from furniture, toys, and wall units to pipes and small household implements like bowls and cutting boards. One of the less fortunate aspects of this position of prestige has been a steadily growing myth about what is typical of Scandinavian design. The consumer has been led to believe, for example, that such commercial labels as "Danish modern" or "Swedish modern" actually represent a specific style in furniture—something that is not now, and never has been, true. The furniture forms made in Scandinavia vary as much in style and in execution as those designed, say, in the United States. What *is* "Scandinavian" about wood forms from Scandinavia is, quite simply, the common-sense, rational, and intelligent way in which they solve problems of environment.

At present wood is not usually included among the fashionable craft materials in contemporary design. On the other hand, for those who dig below the surface of fashion, wood provides a medium of infinite potential, and one that is constantly changing and maturing. For example, laminated and compressed woods, both products of industry, have opened up whole new areas in furniture construction, and these are but two of many new directions in Scandinavian design. What you will see in the pages that follow are illustrations of Scandinavian ingenuity in creating wood forms. This book is offered as vigorous evidence in support of woodcraft, past, present, and future.

WHAT IS DESIGN?

Before there is a problem, there must first of all be a need. All wood form grows out of human need, and the development of that form will vary according to the intensity of the need that gave it birth. To prove a point, let us compare two very dissimilar objects—the Lapp milking bowl and the ordinary chair.

At some undetermined date in early Lapp history, someone discovered that reindeer milk was as nourishing for humans as it was for the reindeer fawn. Thus the Lapp developed the need for a container to extract reindeer milk. Let us suppose that he picked up a chunk of wood and fashioned a bowl with a long handle—and the bowl worked. With the long handle, the bowl could be extended under the doe to catch the milk, and it could even be used afterward as a drinking vessel. Other Lapps must have soon caught on, for the use of reindeer milk and the milking bowl spread throughout the tribes of the Finnmark. And today, because the Lapp still lives in a close, isolated culture, the form is virtually the same as it was many generations ago.

The development of a chair followed quite another course. Once again it is impossible to date the construction of the first chair, but we do know that the earliest ones looked much more like low milking stools than the styles we are familiar with today. At any rate, it is not difficult to understand the need for a chair—it has obvious advantages over sitting on your haunches on a cold floor.

The chair is not a specialized object like the milking bowl. It was and is something to be enjoyed by all people. Naturally, as its use spread throughout the world, it evolved and mutated somewhat the way creatures do as they adapt to different environments. The initial changes in the shape of the chair had nothing to do with beauty or style—they were made to satisfy man's basic need for comfort. The rest came later when man had developed more sophistication.

If you are a very discerning reader, this brief survey may have suggested to you the beginnings of a very important problem in semantics. And you'd be quite correct. Some people have now reached a point of such supersophistication in their attitude toward objects around them that they feel compelled to distinguish between those that are *crafted* and those that are *designed.* This type of labeling has split woodcraft right down the middle. For example, a man making toys, pipes, or games, or whittling household objects out of wood is called simply a craftsman, but an architect building a bed, a wall unit, or a table is called a designer or a designer-craftsman. The implications are obvious: the work of the designer is considered to be much more sophisticated than that of the craftsman.

In this book there has been no attempt to separate design from craft, because I for one don't care a hoot *what* an object is called—if it works then it is justified. This book is about wood, its problems and its great potential in contemporary design. And as far as I'm concerned, a well-executed milking bowl is every bit as sophisticated— and professional—as the most modern of wall units.

Anyone who is upset by my brazen lack of sophistication is invited to hack off a birch burl and carve out a milking bowl that is as good-looking and as functional as the one made by the Lapp. I doubt that afterward he will be able to say that the creative energy required for that feat is any less subtle than the energy required to bolt or glue the parts of a chair together!

DESIGNING MAN'S ENVIRONMENT

THE CHALLENGE OF WOOD   The use of wood dates from the invention of the first crude tool. Since then, pieces of wood have been carved, bent, whittled, glued, nailed, screwed, pegged, and mortised into just about every conceivable object known to man. No other natural material has proved itself so versatile, essential, and challenging.

You have only to look about you to realize the importance of wood in man's environment. The average person, for example, comes home to a wooden or partially wooden house, he sits down on a wooden chair at a wooden table, and he eats food prepared with wooden implements. Later he heaps wooden logs in his fireplace, lights his wooden pipe, and settles down to read his wood-by-product newspaper or to listen to music or news coming out of a wood-encased box. And at day's end, he and his family curl up to sleep in wooden beds.

Considering all this, it hardly seems possible that man could exist without wood. Nevertheless, wood is taken for granted and is seldom given equal critical rank nowadays with plastic, stainless steel, and poured concrete—all very popular materials in contemporary design. Publications on decorating and crafts rarely devote enough space to new work in wood, and students and architects are too often distracted by current fads for this or that "in" material to invest energy exploring wood.

The forms on these pages were made by a small group of dedicated craftsmen and architects, but there is no reason why they could not have been built in the average home workshop. The skills involved in making such forms are basic to any handicraft—a knowledge of tools, an understanding of the material used, and a respect for fine workmanship. Add to this patience, practice, an eye for form, and some imagination, and you have all the elements of fine design.

MODERN FURNITURE STYLES   Every piece of furniture is in a sense also a piece of sculpture. It has form, it has mass, and it takes up space. A well-designed piece of furniture represents an attempt to *discipline* both the mass itself and the space around it. In other words, such a form does not simply occupy its environment, it harmonizes with it. The underlying principle here would seem to be fairly clear-cut—discipline form and you have spatial harmony—but unfortunately it is not so simple. A nondisciplined form is often visually confusing, but one with too much discipline, that is, a sterile form, is likely to be boring. Between these two extremes lies the well-balanced form—and that's where the craftsman with a discerning eye and imagination comes in.

As I've said, furniture forms are usually born quite simply. A farmer or a herdsman needs a chair to sit on, so he builds something that is plain and that will function just as it was meant to. We'd probably call that form "primitive," but all our sophisticated furniture styles—with their carved lion's feet, embellishments, and endless varieties of doodads and gimcracks—began just as humbly. Right now contemporary furniture design seems to have come full circle back to the honest statement of form—a style which we call *modern,* even though it is much closer to the primitive form I just described than it is to, say, the Victorian style. And the Scandinavian designer has played an important role in this return to the straightforward in wood form because he has always been concerned with intelligent and rational ways of solving problems of environment, and he has been clear-sighted enough to realize that doodads and gimcracks do not necessarily enhance form.

Young people today prefer atmospheres of informality to rooms cluttered with ornate furniture and knickknacks—rooms that are decorative, but not very comfortable. In fact, it is not uncommon to find their rooms outfitted with mattresses and brightly colored pillows instead of conventional beds and chairs. Scandinavian designers have attempted to meet the needs of these younger, more casual buyers with furniture that is streamlined and built closer to the floor. In Figure 40, for example, Ilmari Tapiovaara of Finland has constructed a chair which rests directly on the floor, without legs, and Anders Fasterholt of Denmark has solved the problem with elliptical, laminated wood forms strung with nylon fish line, which rock on the floor (see Figures 70 and 71). Other designers like Axel Thygesen of Denmark have created tables so low that you can dispense with chairs altogether and just sit around them on cushions (see Figure 79). An interesting innovation in bed design is the double-decker by Stephan Gip in Figure 68, which actually functions as a self-contained room within a room.

Another popular trend in modern furniture design is portable furniture with add-on units, all of which can be assembled and taken apart in the home. This offers a solution to the urban apartment dweller who is faced with a severe shortage of space and who may have to move frequently. Parts can be assembled in minutes with the turn of a few screws, or locked together like Lincoln logs, and they can also be interchanged or added on later to liven up a room. Naturally, packing and storage will be much more convenient with collapsible pieces, too. From a purely economic standpoint this type of design is a great boon to the Scandinavian manufacturer, because he can export such items at far lower cost than heavier, more cumbersome items.

Portable furniture is wonderful for children—it is often lightweight enough for the child himself to move, and such pieces can be enlarged and regrouped to meet the needs of a growing family. Sectional units such as the one in Figure 55 can always be increased to accommodate a growing store of records, books, or tape recordings. Similarly, portable office units like the piece in Figure 54 are far more attractive and compact than the usual office paraphernalia and still provide the same space. Tables and chairs that can be stacked (see Figure 6) are also a great boon in coping with too little space—both at home and in the office. In fact, the problem of balance in stacking has been so thoroughly dealt with by the Scandinavian designer that he has actually been able to stack thirty chairs one on top of the other in the space normally allotted to only one!

The hanging chair designed by Nanna and Jørgen Ditzel of Denmark in Figure 15 is another, more classic solution to the problem of conserving floor space. Other variations include the piece designed by Finland's Reino Komulainen in Figure 16 and the unusual suspended bookshelves of Denmark's Jørgen Høj in Figure 59. This last item happens to be made with aluminum and canvas, but it could have been constructed equally well with plywood.

Designs in bentwood by Finland's Alvar Aalto (see Figures 2 through 13) are today prized by collectors all over the world. The same type of form is currently being produced by other master craftsmen in Denmark and Finland, who are finding that laminated plywood is strong yet elastic, and is excellent for obtaining smooth, unbroken surfaces in bentwood design. Designers such as Grete Jalk and Perttu Mentula, for example, are aiming for the total look of sculpture in their striking bentwood chairs (see Figures 41, 42, 43, and 45).

Natural woods are by no means ignored by modern cabinetmakers, and pine is a particular favorite, especially in Norway and Finland. The pine most commonly used has a lively grain and is relatively free from knots and internal imperfections. Most pieces made from pine are left unfinished or simply given a clear, matte finish.

Of course, not all woods are naturally lovely, and paint is an obvious way of disguising a poor grain, especially in laminated and compressed woods. Scandinavian cabinetmakers have been among the most vigorous contributors to the trend toward color in contemporary furniture design, and their brightly painted forms have done much to re-establish wood furniture in the hearts of the young. The table and chairs in Figures C-2 and C-6 are outstanding examples of the way in which color can be used not only to camouflage but to enhance furniture form.

Pigment stains are another method of brightening the dull surfaces of industrial woods, and this treatment is frequently used on compressed wood panels. In the designs of Bard Henriksen (see Figures C-4 and C-3), Norwegian flake-board, which actually is composed of numerous wood chips glued together, has been stained to heighten the pattern in the wood.

Another popular design that originated in Scandinavia is the folding chair with removable seat and back, and Danish designer Mogens Koch is probably one of the originators of this idea. His familiar "director's" chairs are illustrated in Figures 26 and 28, the first in elegant leather and rosewood, and the second, the same fine design in less expensive—and washable—canvas. Other designers whose work in this area is outstanding are Ole Gjerløv-Knudsen (see Figures 24 and 25) and Ivan and Benni Schlechter (see Figure 30), all from Denmark.

CHILDREN'S FURNITURE AND TOYS Creating the right environment for a child is a serious task—and one quite different from the design of furniture for adults. Childhood is, after all, a unique and very special stage in the course of human development, and the designer must work to meet its very definite needs. His aim should be to stimulate the child mentally and physically, and to succeed at this he must know something about the stages in child growth. Actual testing of trial forms on babies, toddlers, and young children is the method particularly recommended here, because it gives the designer a chance to learn firsthand what children are capable of at different ages and, above all, *how* the child perceives the adult world.

Normally, older children will be bored by toys that fascinate the very young, and as they become more aware of their own sex, that will make a difference, too, in their preference for playthings. But a young child may easily become fascinated by a toy that he isn't able to handle properly because it's too big or too intricate. Such an experience will be frustrating or humiliating for him, and he could even get hurt.

In general, young children are attracted to bright colors and whimsical shapes, toys that make little noises, and ones with interesting textures. Thus the designer of playthings for babies and toddlers is free to indulge his fantasy in forms that jump, bump, and roll, that quack and squeak; forms with riotous colors and unusual surfaces, bristles, yarn, and soft fur.

As the child grows older his attention span increases. A toy that doesn't challenge his imagination will soon be abandoned. He is capable of greater manual dexterity with objects like puzzles, and games involving balance, and he can also build blocks with great ingenuity and put together houses, boats, and cars from ready-made parts. Another thing he loves to do now is imitate adults with "grown-up" objects.

Naturally he's as unpredictable and energetic as ever. He not only climbs and swings on playground equipment, but on his own furniture as well. Thus, the forms in his room should be safe, with strong joints and rounded edges and smooth surfaces covered with nontoxic paints.

Wood is an ideal material for children's furniture because it is strong, durable, and lightweight; and the industrial varieties are easily processed and inexpensive. In natural woods, hardwood is generally more suitable than softwood, because softwood may splinter or split when abused. Varieties of hardwood most commonly used for children's forms are birch, beech, oak, cherry, walnut, maple, ash, and elm.

Because a child is unpredictable and because he may do just what he's not supposed to do with an object, his furniture should be not only practical but imaginative, too, like the double bench by Anna Tauriala of Finland in Figure 101. Other examples of children's pieces that really meet the needs of childhood are the enameled chair-stools in Figure 91, the rocker in Figure 115, stacked storage units such as the one in Figure 108, and the bed with drawers that convert into miniature vehicles in Figure 102.

Danish painter Palle Nielsen has done some highly creative work in play activities for children. Recently in Stockholm he conducted an experimental program at the Museum of Modern Art, in which children of all ages were permitted to come and play with boards, nails, rope, and tools that had been left about purposely for them. The results were most encouraging: the youngsters knotted nets and built forts and other small dwellings from these raw materials. Apparently when youngsters are left to themselves their play can be not only imaginative but even highly constructive.

Despite this and all the other things that are known about childhood, poorly designed toys and furniture continue to glut the market. Most of these are flashy, overpriced items meant to tantalize parents who don't realize that what *they* like is not necessarily what their children will like. Of course, parents shouldn't be totally ignored by the designer—after all, they're the buyers. They will be grateful for objects that last, that are convenient to keep clean and store, and things that aren't too expensive. A designer who can come up with forms for children that are practical and durable, and still instructive and entertaining, is making a very valuable contribution to childhood.

LIGHT FIXTURES   One of the most interesting developments in Scandinavian woodcraft for the home is light shades made from thin, translucent panels of wood. Lit or unlit, these shades are strikingly handsome room objects, and illuminated they give the room a soft, mellow glow. They are made in a wide range of shapes, from simple spheres and cylinders to spirals and multifaceted polyhedrons like the ones in Figures 162 and 164. Most of the examples in this book are ceiling shades, but lamps on short legs or graceful wooden bases (see Figure 158) are also being developed.

Pine or balsam is generally used for these shades because it is pliable and can be cut into strips. Obviously the quality of the wood is most important in this type of design: wood must be free from knots and defects. Pieces are generally selected for the beauty of their grain and the contrast between outer configurations and the heartwood. In addition, the craftsman tries to use strips that match grain throughout the form.

Wood used for lampshades must be sliced very thin: strips will range from 2½ to 4 millimeters in thickness, depending on the shape of the design. Geometric shades are joined together with glue, a dovetailed mortise and tenon, or small pegs. Many of the very intricate, curved shades, such as the one in Figure 166, are made up of arc strips which have been bonded with wood glue and then clamped at points of juncture with clothespins. For very sharp curves in lamp forms it is necessary to soak the wood in hot water first or steam it at the bending point.

Other shades are woven with these very thin panels of wood. Strips for weaving are also soaked in hot water to make them pliable, and forms are woven freely or over a core—sometimes a large bottle —which is removed when the shade is complete. Scandinavian craftsmen usually begin and end strips on the inside of the forms, tucking them in one under the other instead of gluing them, and then trim the ragged edges with a knife. All the shades illustrated in this book have been left natural or stained with a very thin, nonflammable wood stain that just heightens the grain slightly.

If you'd like to make one of these shades yourself, begin first with a model in tag board or heavy paper. Plan your shade in terms of the type of light you want: direct, indirect, or incidental; and also remember that an opening must be left at the top so that heat from the bulb can escape and the shade won't burn. Be sure, too, that no part of the bulb will actually touch the wood. When you have tested and refined your model, then you can go to work on the actual wooden one, but remember that your craftsmanship here is of supreme importance. Any mistake in construction will immediately be advertised when you turn the lights on!

SOME BASIC PROBLEMS IN WOODCRAFT After looking at so many different styles in Scandinavian design, perhaps we can make some reasonably safe generalizations about the way craftsmen there *conceive of* form, but we would be hard put to find a method of construction that applies in every case. There are those who feel that the method of construction is a relatively unimportant thing—it's the form itself that counts—and those who feel quite oppositely that a piece handcrafted with loving care will be far superior to anything that has been factory-made. Here is how craftsman James Kerenov of Sweden views the issue:

"What we make should, in a personal way, tell about our work—the doing. I am on a dangerous path and I know it. Some people will think I am proposing that we be deliberately naive or primitive. Wrong. Or that our work should be more contemplative, dwelling on details and techniques to the extreme. Wrong again. What occupies me is a search for breadth of expression without manipulation and mannerism—through patience . . . a kind of listening. Maybe I am out of step with the times, I don't know? But must we all be in step? Isn't there a place for those who want to pause . . . and to listen?"

However it's made and whatever it looks like, one thing is certain:

furniture is meant to be used. So if it's not functional, it's not good. Everyone has seen, or has had to use, a poorly designed piece of furniture—something spawned by an architect or designer who should have known better, but who let his imagination run wild. The worst offenders in this respect, however, are beginning students who are so eager to give the world fantastic new forms that they forget practical considerations. The rector of the design school in Bergen, Norway, has told me of a very effective way he has of pounding reality into some of these unfortunately thick heads. His first assignment to students is to design a chair—a chair that they will then sit upon during their entire stay at the school. Students who don't heed the warning in this assignment the first time around usually see the light after a few backaches. Needless to say, their second or third efforts are more careful.

There are no gimmicks in woodcraft. A piece of furniture usually begins as an idea—a mental image that is then transferred to the drawing board or turned into a scale model in wood or cardboard. It is at this point that the craftsman really begins to grapple with the technical problems in his design. How will it be put together: should the joints be concealed or exposed? Where should the maximum strength lie? How will it balance and what will it weigh? Will there be any sharp edges? Will the laminations hold up under stress? Will the moving parts really move the way they should? Will there be hardware, and, if so, what kind? What's the best finish to keep the surface free of scratches and nicks? As he studies his diagram or model, he changes it and refines it. And only after the idea has been fully developed does he proceed to assemble his full-sized form.

It would be impossible in a text of this length to cover step-by-step all the techniques that are used by Scandinavian craftsmen in their work, but we can go into the workshop of two of its leading men and perhaps learn a few things about construction from their methods. The first, Alvar Aalto of Finland, has been doing his well-known work with bentwood with craftsmen at the Kornhonen woodworking studio at Turku. His stools, illustrated in Figures 2 through 10, are made from clear birch that is cut straight from the log and then roughed into shape. Before the legs are bent, five slits of varying depth are cut into them with a table saw at the bend area to reduce the likelihood of cracking and to relieve internal pressure. Thin pieces of birch veneer are then coated with hot glue and forced into the slits, and legs are bent against a curved form and allowed to set. Glued surfaces are then scraped with a thin steel plate to remove excess glue; the legs are trimmed, and finally they are attached to the chair with glued wooden pegs. If screws are used, they are coated with paste soap before being put into the wood to reduce the possibility of tearing and also to seal the area around the insertion. Forms are finished with three coats of clear plastic resin, sprayed on, and before and after each coat they are handrubbed with fine sandpaper. Incidentally, the glue used in the Korhonen workshop is Kaurit 100, Garbamid type, manufactured in West Germany, but available in the United States; and the plastic resin finish used is Natural Plast, a product of Sweden.

Bentwood wall forms in Figures 11 through 13 are also made with slits, but the bends are made cold, that is, without steam, by clamping and rolling. This is particularly hard on the wood, and Mr. Korhonen tells me that although his craftsmen have been doing it for over thirty years, they still have occasional failures. Most of these, he assured me, however, were due to imperfections in the wood rather than human error.

Tapio Wirkkala, a Finnish designer, has done some wild experiments in topographical relief with laminated wood, in a style he has dubbed "rhythmical veneer." To achieve his unusual effects, Mr. Wirkkala incorporates lamination lines into his overall composition. He uses thick blocks of birch veneer, completely knot-free and film-glued under pressure at 90 kilograms (approximately 199 pounds) per square centimeter. Each layer of veneer is very thin, from .1 to 2 millimeters thick, and a lot of wood is used up in the process. "Ultima Thule" (Figures 87 and 88), for example, consumed the equivalent of 10 hectares (approximately 27 acres) of birch veneer, weighing over 5 tons. And of that amount, some 2 tons were carved away by machine.

Mr. Wirkkala knows how to operate the machines used on his forms, and what he doesn't do himself he supervises carefully. In this respect he is like so many other Scandinavian architects and designers who have had and continue to have practical experience working in their medium, even as professionals. Perhaps this is one of the reasons for the continuing quality and excellence of Scandinavian design.

This has been, as I promised, a *brief* study of techniques. If the reader desires more instruction he is invited to study the pictures—they contain a wealth of information in a form far more graphic than words. Any of the books and periodicals listed in Materials for Further Study will also be of great help to the would-be craftsman, and those who wish to correspond directly with the designers featured here can obtain their addresses through the craft societies listed at the back.

DECORATIVE WOODCRAFT

Holiday ornaments, handsome cutlery and kitchenware, mobiles, jewelry, pipes—these are a few of the myriad of decorative wooden articles besides furniture for which the Scandinavian craftsman is noted. Perhaps he, more than any other craftsman in any other place, has recognized the enormous potential of wood for unique design in different areas. And in his hands even the simplest of objects can suddenly be turned into an exciting form.

Take the case of Kaija Aarikka, a Finnish designer who began her career in textiles. Few Finns today will probably remember the dresses that Mrs. Aarikka created, but none has forgotten the wooden buttons, made out of lively, colorful beads, that adorned these dresses. The success of her buttons put Mrs. Aarikka into the button business, and it wasn't long before she had expanded into candleholders trimmed with beads, earrings, necklaces, bracelets, and belts, beaded children's toys, and even room screens. Today her workshop contains several dozen craftsmen, and she supplies her own shops in major European cities and also exports her designs all over the world. All this because she had an eye for form and a little ingenuity. Designers who are so busy creating immortal works of art that they haven't time to bother with anything as mundane as the bead might take notice of Mrs. Aarikka's success. They might consider, too, that her creations are providing thousands everywhere with a great deal of pleasure.

HOLIDAY WOOD FORMS   A holiday celebration in Scandinavia is invariably accompanied by festive ornaments for the house. At Christmas, for example, it is customary to highlight the festivities with the St. Thomas cross, doves, angels, and roosters, all fashioned exquisitely of wood; and to use fragrant juniper bowls and platters for food and handsome bentwood decorations on the wall. Painstaking care goes into preparation of all these holiday forms. The cross illustrated in Figure 203, a classic form, has been made from two very straight-grained pieces of soft wood—usually it is pine or balsam—delicately feathered and curled with a knife to form the whorled patterns you see. In the case of the angel and dove in Figure 205, the feathers are fanned out instead of curled. All three forms are left unfinished.

Use of strong, pleasant-smelling juniper wood is a special tradition among the Finns, and at Christmas the Stockmann Department Store in Helsinki sells thousands of small slices of juniper, along with strips of pine lattice, to Finns who will make their own forms and thus bring a little personal creativity into their homes during the Christmas season. The inlaid plate and the hot plate illustrated in Figure 210 are made with thin-sliced, cross-grained juniper pieces. The same material is also used for wall decorations and for larger items such as screens and room dividers.

Finnish designer Sirkka Forrs is responsible for the intriguing wall decorations featured in Figures C-10 through C-12. To make these forms she uses pine shavings about ½ inch wide and 1½ to 2 millimeters thick, soaking them first to render them soft and pliable. She bends the shavings into form, applying a few spots of glue to hold them intact. Once set, the forms are dipped into dye.

PIPES The craftsmen of Denmark remain the unchallenged masters of imaginative form and technical skill in pipe-making. Handmade pipes from Denmark range from the conventional bowl type to free-form sculpture of the type illustrated in Figures 213 through 216 and pipes have been fashioned from all sorts of materials—including corn cob and clay. The most respected bowl among discerning pipe-smokers is made from the root of the low, prickly brier shrub *(Erica arborea)* found in southern Europe, particularly Greece and Corsica. This root is dense, with a lively grain figure that offers limitless potential for sculpture. As a pipe, it produces a mild, even-burning smoke.

The brier root is seasoned slowly in pipe-making, and aged with the same care as good wine or whiskey—often for as long as one hundred years. Properly aged brier is obtained already cut into small blocks the approximate size of the bowl. It is first bathed in steam for several hours to prevent it cracking later on, and then dried out slowly at room temperature. (Brier must never be force-dried.) Now the pipe is ready to be formed.

An average pipe consists of the bowl, made from the brier wood; the stem or shank; and the mouthpiece or bit. Before the bowl is shaped, the craftsman usually spends a good deal of time studying the grain figure of his block, and very often he will let the grain suggest the bowl form. This form should not only balance well in the hand, but its grain should blend evenly with that of the shank. The pipe-maker will then draw the form on the block (see Figure 211) and carve it out. To allow himself complete freedom of design, the pipe-maker usually carves out the entire bowl form before he makes any holes for stem and tobacco.

The bowl is sanded to velvety smoothness with grades of sandpaper from rough to fine, and then, when the grain surface is fully exposed, the pipe-maker decides on the color for his pipe. It may be left natural or treated with a chemical, wood-tone dye that has been specially prepared for pipes. Often the tones are developed progressively with several dyes, and the form is resanded after each dye tone is induced. Finally, the outside surface of the bowl is coated with a thin layer of paste wax, usually Carnauba, and then either heated gently or polished hard to spread the wax into a thin veneer. Varnish has not been used on any of the pipes you see here; it is considered to be in bad taste by most professional pipe-makers.

After the mouthpiece has been added to the bowl, the inside is coated with a special mixture of charcoal and sugar, which will insulate the brier from the first few break-in burnings. Each pipe-maker usually has developed his own special formula, and with the right mixture the brier will burn just a little, but not too much. After a few smokings, the pipe forms its own natural insulation.

Pipe-makers can vary the surface on their pipe bowls by sandblasting the sides to roughen them, or preserving the natural surface of the brier block at the top, sides, or base, as you see in Figures 213 and 214. The techniques, as well as all the pipes described in this text, are courtesy of Ole W. O. Larsen of Denmark, proprietor of a pipeshop in Copenhagen that has been in his family since 1864. The bowls and half of the stems on these Larsen pipes are all fashioned out of one piece of brier because Mr. Larsen feels the lines of the bowl form should remain uninterrupted. The remaining portion of these Larsen pipe stems are made either from horn—particularly buffalo horn—or bamboo or Vulcanite, and the mouthpiece is also of Vulcanite, a rubber-like composition that resists denting and moisture.

A final note on the Danish pipe-maker: his background is often unusual. One of Mr. Larsen's pipe-makers, for example, is a housewife who specializes in mending broken pipes, and another began as a machinist. Still another was a carpenter who started by whittling small wooden models. But all of them, however they started, share a common respect for meticulous craftsmanship and attention to detail—two very basic demands of pipe-making.

LAPP WOODCRAFT   Lapland is that area in Scandinavia which comprises northern Norway, Sweden, Finland, and the northwestern corner of Russia. Once it was a culture known for its handicrafts—fine work in horn and bone, woven fabrics and basketry, tin-thread embroidery, and, of course, wood. The Lapp perfected these crafts to survive. His climate was extreme, and he and his reindeer herd roamed the moors of Finnmark constantly in search of food. Such a life barred him from the luxury of a fixed residence or numerous possessions, so the Lapp learned to improvise, to make his objects as he went, and to take advantage of whatever natural materials were available to him. With knife and axe he fashioned from the native birch, mountain ash, alder, and sallow, and from the horn and bone obtained from his herd, all the implements necessary to his life: bowls, cups, canteens, salt flasks, buckets, baskets, boxes, even his *akja*—the curved, boatlike sledge in which he rode behind his reindeer.

Today these ancient folk arts are in grave danger of dying out because the once-industrious Lapp has been made idle by government funds. This money was intended to encourage the continuance of Lapp customs, but, unfortunately, it is being doled out to him like charity—and has turned him into a kind of tourist attraction. To make matters worse, forms that had always been handcrafted by the Lapp are now being made outside of Lapland. The traditional Lapp costume, for example, is now imported by the Lapp from Austria!

This is indeed a tragedy, but the situation is not entirely lost. Although there are fewer than a dozen master craftsmen still living in Lapland—most of them centered in Jokkmakk in Swedish Lapland—in *their* work, at least, has survived the infinite patience, the concern for detail, and the meticulous craftsmanship characteristic of Lapp work of old. The Lapp sensitivity for form has been beautifully expressed by Swedish writer Gunilla Lundahl, who, together with Swedish photographer Pal-Nils Nilsson, has been studying Lapp culture for many years. Miss Lundahl writes:

"*Dakkan* is the Lapp word meaning to make with your hands, or caress with kindness. It can serve as a symbol for Lapp art handicraft. This handicraft exhibits a form language which reflects a style of life in more than one way. It displays a soft, smiling, and light form-world, in tune with nature, kind to the hand, and an integral part of a way of life. It shows how an inexhaustible fund of experience, material know-how, adaptation to function, and a living feeling for form can easily be turned toward new discoveries, new expressions, and new uses."*

By "new discoveries, new expressions, and new uses" Miss Lundahl means contemporary redefinitions of traditional forms, such as the door pulls by Esse Poggats in Figure 219, which were inspired by a Lapp magic-drum handle. A variation of the same form, also by Mr. Poggats, is the carry-all with engraved horn handle in Figure 220.

Lapp craftsmen have always been particularly attracted to tree

* From "Lapp Handicraft," *Kontur Swedish Design Annual,* 1965, p. 38.

burl in their woodcraft because it has an exotic grain figure and is also extremely dense and therefore durable. In Figure 232, designer Poggats is seen attacking an enormous birch burl with his axe. He later fashioned this into a bowl.

The Swedish Lapp will generally secure burl from the beech or birch, but the Finn prefers digging up the burl root of the raita—a willow variety harder than birch. The *naappu,* the reindeer milking bowl, and the *kuksa,* a drinking cup, in Figure 229 are both made from this raita burl. After the burl was cut from the root it was divided into blocks approximately the size of the intended forms, and the holes for the cup and the outside lines of the form were roughed in while the wood was still fresh and green. This initial heavy work is done on green wood to avoid the chance of cracking later on. Completed cup and bowl were smoothed on a grindstone and then finished with fine sandpaper. No varnish or finish coat was used because this particular burl is so dense it sheds water like a stone.

Craftsmen at the Lauri workshop, where these forms were made, use power tools, but many Lapps still prefer the axe for rough work and the gouge for finer work. In fact, one Lapp craftsman was observed using a very primitive but still highly functional neck sling made from rawhide. Such a sling hangs to the waist and is wrapped around the shaft of a gouge so that when it is swung the sling acts as a pivot, directing the tool toward the wood.

Root and bark are used by Lapp craftsmen to weave baskets like the one in Figure 233, made from root fiber gathered from the moors, then drawn, washed, and boiled. Bark baskets are generally made from strips of birch bark, sized on the tree trunk, and then peeled downward off the tree with a dull wooden implement similar to a putty knife. These baskets are not as strong or tight as the root type, and if the bark is not woven immediately it must be kept soft and pliable in hot water. Neither root nor bark baskets are finished—indeed, the Lapp seems to prefer a natural surface on most of his forms.

Engraved reindeer horn is often used to inlay wooden implements by the Lapp, the soft, creamy tones of the horn contrasting handsomely with the burnished wood. When reindeer horn is freshly cut it is pinkish in color, but it turns greener by degrees as it ages. To obtain the eggshell color he prefers, the Lapp craftsman will generally blanch his horn in a stream—often for as long as three years—and then dry it in the sun. Blanched horn is engraved with a knife or X-acto blade (in one instance, I found a Lapp craftsman using an old dentist's drill), and cuts are rubbed first with powdered alder bark and then with sedge grass to highlight and smooth engravings. Outstanding examples of this inlaid Lapp work include the knife in Figure 224 and the box in Figure 227.

As you see, although the Lapp craftsmen are few in number, they are carrying on their traditions in magnificent fashion. Happily, authentic Lapp crafts are valued throughout Scandinavia as great works of art—and rightly so, they are that good.

C-1. "Double-decker" by Stephen Gip of Sweden. This eight-sided form is made from hinged wood panels that are laminated with plastic resin. The unit stands 57 inches high, with a sleeping or sitting unit on the top. Mr. Gip feels that the human body needs room to fidget, stretch, and turn. This form is his solution to body confinement. (Courtesy of Tiofoto Bildbyra Ab.)

C-2

C-3

C-4

C-2. Enameled, bent-plywood chair with matching table. By Mona Kinn of Norway. (Courtesy of *Bonytt* magazine.)

C-3. Table and armchairs made of stained Norwegian flake-board. By Bard Henriksen of Denmark. (Courtesy of Møbel-Fiske, Surnadal, Norway.)

C-4. Double-decker bed, storage, and study unit by Bard Henriksen of Denmark. The unit is made of Norwegian "flake-board," a compressed panel of wood chips, and is stained with lacquer. The unit may be taken apart for shipment and reassembled with screws. The ladder holes for the elevated bed are lined with plastic. (Courtesy of Møbel-Fiske, Surnadal, Norway.)

C-7. Element shelves in painted birch.
By Rintala of Finland.

C-5

C-6

C-7

C-8. Ceiling shade from pine splintwood by Hans Agne-Jakobsson of Sweden.

C-9. Table lamp of pine splintwood by Hans-Agne Jakobsson of Sweden. The lamp is about 10 inches high and was made by stacking rings concentrically.

C-10. Holiday rooster by Sirkka Forss of Finland. Form is made from thin shavings of pine that were soaked and bent. (Courtesy of A. B. Norna Oy.)

C-11. "Eve Flower," "Citrus," and "Steak-Stick" by Sirkka Forss of Finland. Forms are made from thin shavings of pine that were soaked and bent. (Courtesy of A. B. Norna Oy.)

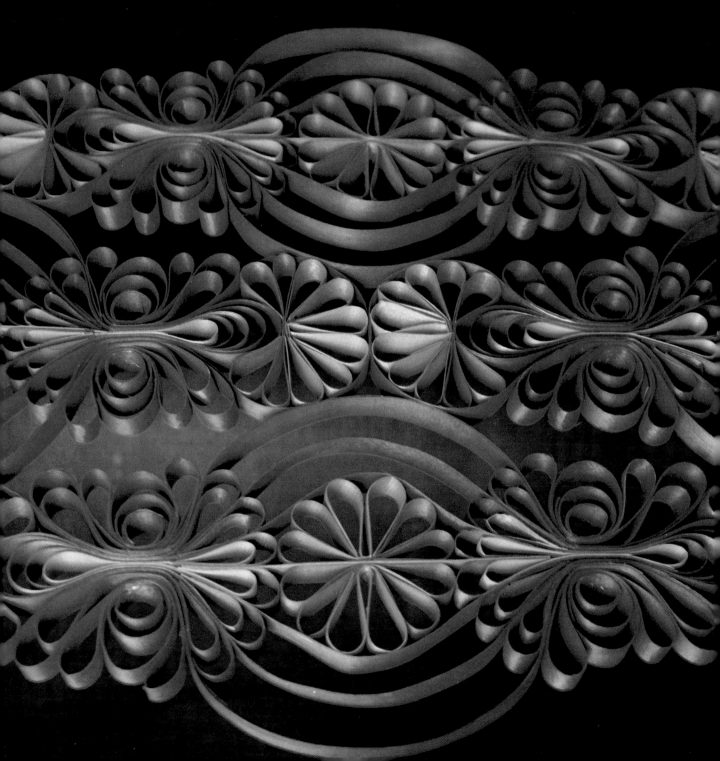

FURNITURE

1. Pine chair handmade in Finland in the early nineteenth century. (Courtesy of the National Museum of Finland.)

1

C-12. Wall decoration by Sirkka Forss of Finland. Form is made of thin pine shavings that were soaked and bent into form. After the forms were set with glue, the piece was dunked in stain. (Courtesy of A. B. Norna Oy.)

2. Three stools by Alvar Aalto of Finland, using negative space in the leg bend. Lower stool is designed for use in the sauna. Stool legs are made from birch and reinforced with strips of birch veneer at the bend area. (Courtesy of Artek.)

3. Bent-leg stool by Alvar Aalto of Finland. The leg is birch, and the seat is leather-covered ash. (Courtesy of Artek.)

4. Bentwood leg form by Alvar Aalto of Finland. The bend is reinforced with laminated strips of birch. (Courtesy of Artek.)

6

5. Clamping the birch rim on the stacking-stool seat. (Courtesy of Alvar Aalto and Artek.)

6. Stacking stools in birch by Alvar Aalto of Finland. (Courtesy of Artek.)

7. High stool in birch, with laminated and molded back. By Alvar Aalto of Finland. Mr. Aalto designed a basic leg that could be used on a number of chair and stool forms. (Courtesy of Artek.)

7

8. Inserting ⅛ inch thick birch veneer slats into bend area of Aalto leg. Slats are first dipped in glue and then forced into slits cut into the chair leg. (Courtesy of Korhonen Oy.)

9. Birch chair by Alvar Aalto of Finland. Form was designed for stacking, using the same basic, interchangeable leg. (Courtesy of Artek.)

10. Detail of Aalto bent-leg in birch, with birch veneer laminations at the bend area. (Courtesy of Artek.)

8

9

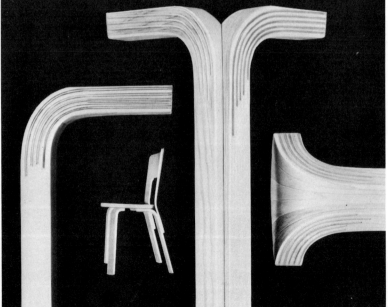

10

11. Laminated and bent form in birch by Alvar Aalto of Finland. The form is used for wall shelf brackets and also on umbrella stands. The bend is made cold, with one continuous piece of laminated birch. (Courtesy of Korhonen Oy.)

12. Clamping and rolling the cold bend on the triangular birch wall bracket in Figure 12. By Alvar Aalto of Finland. (Courtesy of Korhonen Oy.)

13. Continuing the cold bend on the wall bracket. (Courtesy of Korhonen Oy.)

12

13

14. Ash stool with screw-in legs by Mogens Lassen of Denmark. Form was turned. (Courtesy of K. Thomsen and the Danish Society of Arts, Crafts, and Industrial Design.)

15. Hanging chair in basket weave by Nanna and Jørgen Ditzel of Denmark. (Courtesy of R. Wengler and the Danish Society of Arts, Crafts, and Industrial Design.)

16. Hanging chair in cane by Reino Komulainen of Finland. (Courtesy of Maija-Liisa Komulainen.)

14

15

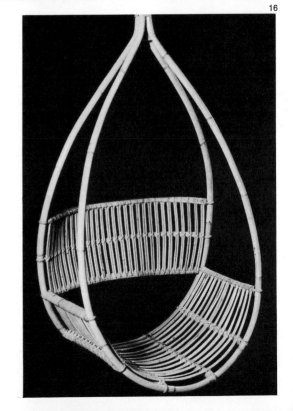

16

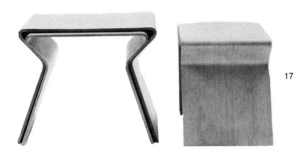

17. Laminated bentwood stool by Grete Jalk of Denmark. (Courtesy of P. Jeppesen and the Danish Society of Arts, Crafts, and Industrial Design.)

18. Cane chair by Maija-Liisa Komulainen of Finland. (Courtesy of Reino Komulainen.)

19. Sauna stool by Antti Nurmesniemi of Finland. Seat is formed from laminated birch veneer. (Courtesy of A. Liljamaa and the Finnish Society of Arts and Crafts.)

20. Wall chairs in pitch pine and canvas
by Peter Ole Schionning of Denmark. Chairs
are bracketed right onto the wall.
(Courtesy of Johannes Hansen.)

21. Pine stool by Oy Stockmann of Finland.
(Courtesy of the Finnish Design Center.)

22. Unfinished sauna bench by Perttu Mentula
of Finland. (Courtesy of Velsa Oy and the
Finnish Design Center.)

20

21

22

23. Chair in ash, with slip-on canvas seat and back. By Ditte and Adrian Heath of Denmark. (Courtesy of Cadovius and the Danish Society of Arts, Crafts, and Industrial Design.)

24. Beech-and-canvas collapsible chair by Ole Gjerløv-Knudsen of Denmark. The canvas is loosened and slipped off the beech posts. The whole unit comes apart and can be wrapped up in its own canvas. (Courtesy of Interna.)

25. Beech-and-canvas collapsible chair by Ole Gjerløv-Knudsen of Denmark. Tension can be adjusted by twisting the stretcher rope that spans the two front legs. This is the same method that is used on an ordinary bucksaw. (Courtesy of Interna.)

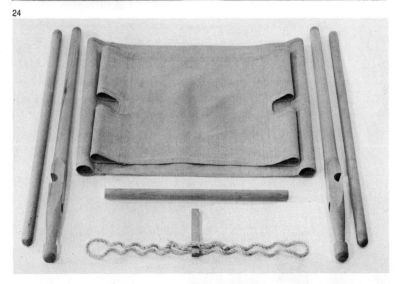

24

25

26. Rosewood-and-leather folding chair by Mogens Koch of Denmark. The chair has solid brass findings and folds by pulling up on the seat. This form was designed in 1933, but it is still one of the most popular Danish export items. (Courtesy of Interna.)

27. Collapsible chair, stool, and table using canvas, birch, and rope. By Erik Magnussen of Denmark. The rope threads a pin that is turned to secure proper tension. Chairs and stool can be taken apart and carried in a small, convenient package. (Courtesy of Dansk Hardwood and the Danish Society of Arts, Crafts, and Industrial Design.)

28. Beech-and-linen canvas folding chair by Mogens Koch of Denmark. This is a less expensive version of the rosewood and leather chair illustrated in 26. In this view is illustrated how the form is folded and stored in a rack specially designed for the chair. (Courtesy of Interna.)

26

27

28

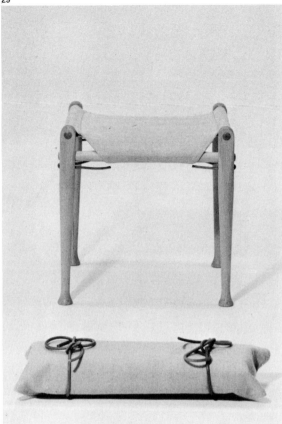

29. Beech-and-linen canvas folding stool by Axel Thygesen of Denmark. (Courtesy of Interna.)

30. Beech-and-hemp canvas chairs by Ivan and Benni Schlechter of Denmark. These forms are not only collapsible but convertible and can be combined into one, two, and three units. Hemp canvas bags are drawn down over the beech frame to form the back and arm rests.

31. Laminated beech chair with leather by Ingmar Relling of Norway. The stool seat and the seat and back of the chair are laced with canvas to support the leather cushions. The chair is also made in a less expensive beech and canvas model. (Courtesy of Vestlandske Møbelfabrikk A/S and the Norsk Design Centrum.)

31

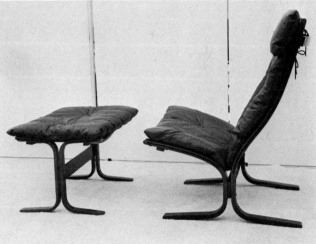

30

32. Collapsible safari chair in birch, with either canvas or leather covering. By Norrmark Handicraft of Finland. Stretchers are held to the legs with dowel pins.

33. Two bent forms of laminated oak make up the frame for this chair by Svein Mortensen of Norway. Seats are available in either canvas or tufted wool. (Courtesy of Sørliemøbler A/S.)

34. Safari chair (detail) showing how the covering is belted in place with straps and buckles. Chair is so compact that it can be fitted into a large suitcase. (Courtesy of Norrmark Handicraft of Finland.)

35. Front view of clear pine chair pegged together with mortise and tenon. By Edvin Helseth of Norway. This simple form in unfinished pine won the 1968 Better Living Award in Scandinavia. (Courtesy of Trybo.)

36. Side view of pine chair by Edvin Helseth of Norway. The chair seat and back are curved to fit the human form. (Courtesy of Trybo.)

37. Viking chair with birch frame and woven rope seat. By Jørken Høvelskov of Denmark. (Courtesy of Den Permanente and Christensen and Larsen.)

37

38. Molded plywood chair showing various woven seat backs. By Peter Karpf of Denmark. (Courtesy of Christensen and Larsen and the Danish Society of Arts, Crafts, and Industrial Design.)

39. "Korento," chair in bleached birch with seat base of bent birch plywood. Form designed by Tanu Toiviainen of Finland. (Courtesy of Sotka Oy.)

40. "Porpoise" by Ilmari Tapiovaara of Finland. Oak form rests without legs directly on the floor and is covered with a stretch nylon cushion. (Courtesy of Oy Skaano Ab.)

38

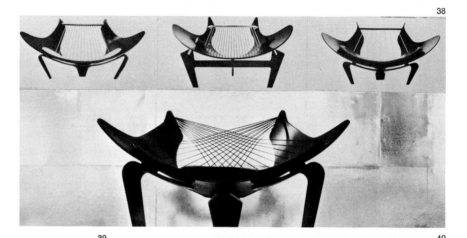

39

40

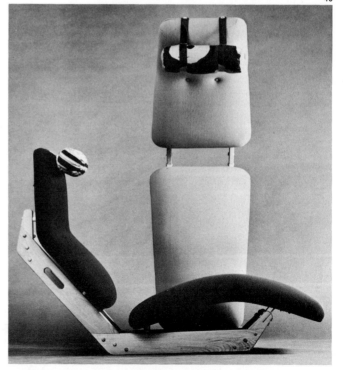

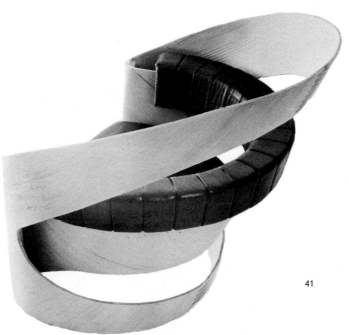

41. Bent plywood chair with leather cushion by Grete Jalk of Denmark. (Courtesy of the Danish Society of Arts, Crafts, and Industrial Design.)

42. Laminated and bent oak chair by Grete Jalk of Denmark. (Courtesy of the Danish Society of Arts, Crafts, and Industrial Design.)

41

42

43. "Thiller," enamel-painted, bent plywood chair by Perttu Mentula of Finland. Seat cushion is supported by nylon rope woven into plywood frame. (Courtesy of Peem Oy.)

44. Molded oak-plywood chair with chrome legs. By Arne Jacobsen of Denmark. (Courtesy of Fritz Hansen and the Danish Society of Arts, Crafts, and Industrial Design.)

45. "Thiller" (top and back view) by Perttu Mentula of Finland.

43

45

44

46

46. Collapsible chair in unfinished fir plywood by Aksel Dahl of Denmark. Tongue and groove lock seat and back in place. Cushion is held in place by a dowel, and the arms and back are pushed through slots in the side of the chair frame. (Courtesy of Rud. Rasmussen and the Danish Society of Arts, Crafts, and Industrial Design.)

47. Bent plywood chairs in beech by Rastad and Relling of Norway. (Courtesy of A/S Futurum.)

47

48. "Vanikka" by Kristian Gullichsen of Finland. This series consists of a table in six different sizes, a stool, an armchair, a sofa, a low table, and a child's chair. All pieces in the series have the same construction: collapsible 12-millimeter birch plywood, held together with brass screws and brackets. The plywood is painted. (Courtesy of Norrmark Handicraft.)

49. Rocking-bowl chair with canvas sides by Peter Karpf of Denmark. Bowl is turned from laminated pitch pine. (Courtesy of Leschly Jacobsen and the Danish Society of Arts, Crafts, and Industrial Design.)

50. "Vanikka" table shown ready to assemble. (Courtesy of Norrmark Handicraft.)

51. "Vanikka" (detail). (Courtesy of Norrmark Handicraft.)

48

49

50

51

52. Sofa, armchair, and low table from the "Vanikka" series. (Courtesy of Norrmark Handicraft.)

53. Sectional unit with sawhorse legs and center trestle. By Finn Juhl of Denmark. (Courtesy of the Royal Danish Ministry for Foreign Affairs.)

52

53

54. Home-file unit, available in teak, mahogany, oak, and walnut. By Selfile Systemer A/S of Norway. When closed, this unit measures only 32¼ by 45¼ by 21¼ inches. Opened, it doubles in size, providing the equivalent of an entire office.

55. "Bagdad," sectional boxes in painted birch by Eero Aarnio of Finland. (Courtesy of Peem Oy.)

56. Fold-out bar in walnut by Selfile Systemer A/S of Norway.

54

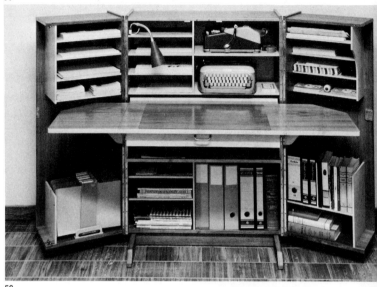

55

56

57. Birch-dowel wine rack by Richard Nissen of Denmark. The plug-in system allows the rack to be fitted into any space available.

58. Birch-dowel wine rack by Richard Nissen of Denmark. The construction of this basic form is similar to that used in Tinker Toys.

59. Suspended book shelves in hemp canvas by Jørgen Høj of Denmark. The forms photographed here are aluminum, but could also have been done in enamel-painted plywood. Shelves collapse for storage and shipment. Weights strapped on the bottom keep the form from turning. (Courtesy of Ivan Schlechter.)

58

59

60. Birch rings used in a restaurant drape. By Kaija Aarikka of Finland.

61. Room-divider screens made of strung birch beads, disks, rods, and slats. By Kaija Aarikka of Finland.

62. Detail of pine beads stained and strung for use in room divider. By Kaija Aarikka of Finland.

60

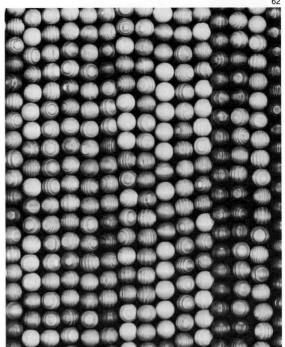

62

61

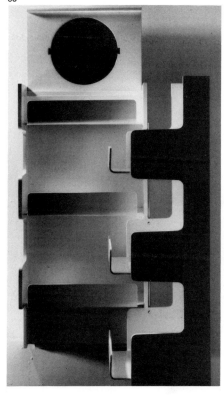

63

64

65

63. Wall chest in Gabon plywood with pigment lacquer surface. By Stig Lonngren, SIR, of Sweden. The chest is opened by swinging the cover out. Both the cover and the wall section are made for storage. (Courtesy of Stig Lonngren and Lars Larsson.)

64. Collapsible room screen in fir plywood by Aksel Dahl of Denmark. Pieces fit together with interlocking tongues and grooves, as shown on the end piece. (Courtesy of Rud. Rasmussen and the Danish Society of Arts, Crafts, and Industrial Design.)

65. Room screen in birch by Alvar Aalto of Finland. (Courtesy of Artek.)

66. Jungle gym tunnel and step unit with painted surface. By Verner Panton of Denmark. (Courtesy of Louis Poulsen and the Danish Society of Arts, Crafts, and Industrial Design.)

67. "Pillow box" by Stephan Gip of Sweden. Piece is made from hinged panel sections covered with laminated plastic resin.

68. Double-decker by Stephan Gip of Sweden. Form is eight-sided, with hinged panel sections covered with laminated plastic resin.

66

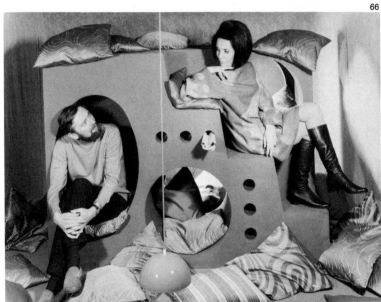

67

68

69

69. Double-decker bunk bed in Norwegian flake-board, made from compressed wood chips. By Bard Henriksen of Denmark. Form is collapsible. (Courtesy of Møbel-Fiske.)

70. Circle rocking floor form by Anders Fasterholt of Denmark. (Courtesy of Christensen and Larsen.)

71. Circle rocking floor form by Anders Fasterholt of Denmark. Frame is made from laminated and bent pitch pine, strung with nylon. (Courtesy of Christensen and Larsen.)

72. Double-decker desk bed in stained Norwegian flake-board. By Bard Henriksen of Denmark. (Courtesy of Møbel-Fiske, Surnadal, Norway.)

70

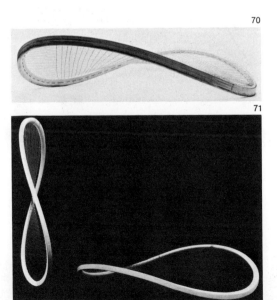

71

72

73. Child's bed in lacquered birch by Lars Morsberg of Sweden. Drawers under bed provide storage space, and when turned over, they serve as steps. (Courtesy of Ragnvald Torkelson and Svenska Slojdforeningen.)

74. Enamel-painted plywood table with inlaid metal tray. By Perttu Mentula of Finland. (Courtesy of Peem Øy.)

75. Painted birch bunk bed designed for stacking. By Pirkko Stenros of Finland. (Courtesy of Muurame and the Finnish Society of Crafts and Design.)

73

74

75

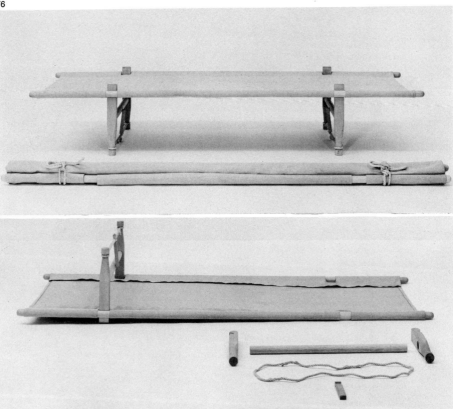

76. Beech-and-canvas folding bed by Ole Gjerløv-Knudsen of Denmark. Bed uses the bucksaw principle for tension. (Courtesy of Interna.)

77. Beech-and-canvas folding bed being assembled. (Courtesy of Interna and Ole Gjerløv-Knudsen.)

78 Beech-and-canvas folding bed (detail) showing how fabric is stretched. (Courtesy of Interna.)

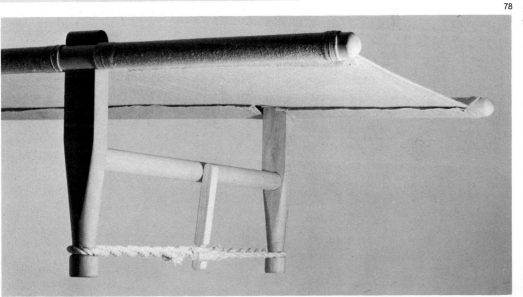

79. Floor table with cushions by Axel Thygesen of Denmark. (Courtesy of Interna and the Danish Society of Arts, Crafts, and Industrial Design.)

80. Birch-plywood folding table with laminated pigment surface. By Stig Lonngren, SIR, of Sweden. (Courtesy of Stig Lonngren and Lars Larsson.)

81. "Prepop," bentwood table and chair in birch. By Arne Jacobsen of Denmark. (Courtesy of Asko of Finland.)

79

80

81

82. Silverware chest in chestnut and pear. By James Krenov of Sweden.

83. Silverware chest (detail) by James Krenov of Sweden.

84. Sea monument in laminated birch veneer by Tapio Wirkkala of Finland.

85. Form in birch veneer by Tapio Wirkkala of Finland. Form is made up of many layers of laminated birch veneer.

86. Form in laminated birch veneer by Tapio Wirkkala of Finland. (Courtesy of the Finnish Society of Crafts and Design.)

84

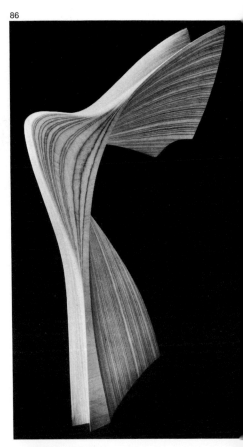

86

85

87. "Ultima Thule" (detail) by Tapio Wirkkala of Finland.

88. "Ultima Thule," topographical relief in laminated birch veneer. Designed by Tapio Wirkkala of Finland for Expo '67. Laminations are film-glued under pressure.

CHILDREN'S FORMS

89. Enameled plywood chair (detail) by Kristian Gullichsen of Finland. Two different seat positions are gained simply by turning the chair upside down. The openings in the sides provide handles for the child to move the chair about. (Courtesy of Norrmark Handicraft.)

90. Birch playroom stools by Norrmark Handicraft of Finland. The low, stubby legs and the scooped seat provide balance and keep the child from sliding off the edge of the seat.

91. Enameled plywood chair by Kristian Gullichsen of Finland. The four pieces in this chair are held together with brackets and screws. The chair is convertible and may be tipped over for an alternate seat height or for use as a small table.

89

90

91

92

93

94

92. Child's chair in laminated beech with adjustable seat. By Kristian Vedel of Denmark. (Courtesy of Torben Ørskov and the Danish Society of Arts, Crafts, and Industrial Design.)

93. Child's bench and table in laminated beech plywood by Jørgen Klinkby of Denmark. The forms are collapsible, with interlocking slits. They can be assembled by the child. (Courtesy of Interna.)

94. Collapsible beech children's furniture finished with clear matte lacquer. By Hans J. Wegner of Denmark. (Courtesy of Salesco and the Danish Society of Arts, Crafts, and Industrial Design.)

95. Four chairs and table in laminated beech plywood (top view) by Kristian Vedel of Denmark. The chair backs are bent to fit the table forms. (Courtesy of Torben Ørskov and the Danish Society of Arts, Crafts, and Industrial Design.)

96. Convertible highchair by Tage Sand of Denmark. Chair lifts off to become a chair and table. (Courtesy of the Danish Society of Arts, Crafts, and Industrial Design.)

97. Crib in laminated birch by Anna Tauriala of Finland. The legs and top rim are bent forms, and the crib is finished with transparent, matte lacquer. (Courtesy of Korhonen Oy.)

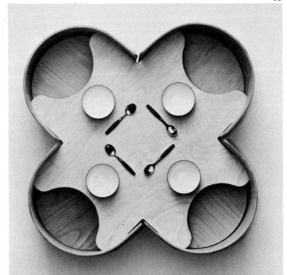

95

96

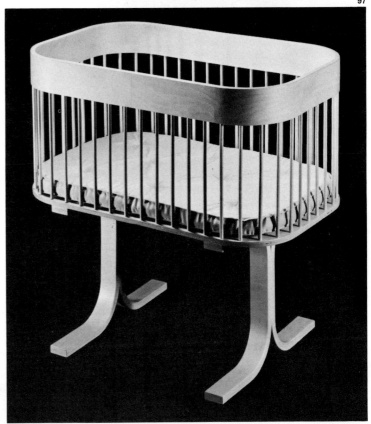

97

98

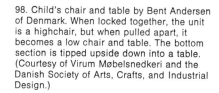

98. Child's chair and table by Bent Andersen of Denmark. When locked together, the unit is a highchair, but when pulled apart, it becomes a low chair and table. The bottom section is tipped upside down into a table. (Courtesy of Virum Møbelsnedkeri and the Danish Society of Arts, Crafts, and Industrial Design.)

99. Child's chair is molded birch plywood with pigment-lacquer finish. By Stig Lonngren, SIR, of Sweden. The plate and seat are detachable, making it possible to stack the center cone. The plate is meant to be hung against the wall when not in use. (Courtesy of Stig Lonngren, Lars Larsson, and Stedelijk Museum of Amsterdam.)

100. Highchair in lacquered birch by Ben af Schulten of Finland. (Courtesy of Norrmark Handicraft.)

99

100

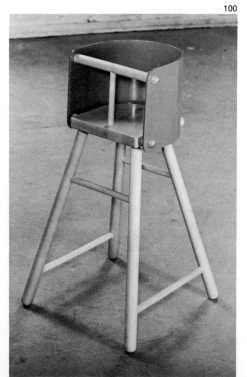

101. Double bench by Anna Tauriala of Finland. The bench is made from 11 layers of laminated birch, bent to form and finished with pigment lacquer. Bench has a variety of other uses. (Courtesy of Korhonen Oy.)

102. Painted-birch child's bed with drawers by Pirkko Stenros of Finland. The drawers under the bed convert into a play car with wheels. (Courtesy of Muurame and the Finnish Society of Crafts and Design.)

103. Children's chairs and table in beech by Kaj Bojesen of Denmark. The chairs come in two sizes and are designed to fit under the table for convenient storage. The steering wheel locks in place to convert chairs into a play vehicle.

101

102

103

104. Double benches shoved together to form tunnels. (Courtesy of Korhonen Oy.)

105. Double benches used as bases for a table. (Courtesy of Korhonen Oy.)

104

105

106. Double bench tipped to the side to form the base of a coffee table (Courtesy of Korhonen Oy.)

107. Double benches with the addition of a plywood molded chute serve as a slide base. (Courtesy of Korhonen Oy.)

108. Model for children's furniture by Flemmig Hvidt of Denmark. As a student at the Danish Handicraft School, Mr. Hvidt designed this form for an international competition sponsored by Childcraft of Salem, Indiana, and took first prize. It is constructed out of birch panels fitted together with pegs and rings. The panels are ½ inch thick and painted with red enamel.

108

106

107

109. Model for children's furniture by
Flemmig Hvidt of Denmark. The locking
arrangement allows for conversion to
bookshelves, a desk unit, a child's bed, and,
with the addition of wheels, a vehicle. The
panels can also be used as a room divider.

110. Model for children's furniture by
Flemmig Hvidt of Denmark (detail). The pin
and ring lock the panels.

111. Model for children's furniture by
Flemmig Hvidt of Denmark (detail). The
wooden cap is screwed into the center pin to
hold the rings in place.

112. Model for children's furniture by
Flemmig Hvidt of Denmark (detail). This
illustrates how the interlocking panels come
together.

110

111

112

113. Canvas-and-dowel playhouse by Lena Larsson of Sweden. The dowels plug into large wooden beads. (Courtesy of Svenska Slojdforeningen.)

114. Single-unit chair, table, and rocking horse by Niels Jørgen of Denmark. This unit may be converted into a rocking horse by turning it on its side. (Courtesy of Poul Jensen and the Danish Society of Arts, Crafts, and Industrial Design.)

115. "Joker," child's rocking form with interchangeable parts. By Borje Lindau and Bo Lindecrantz of Sweden. (Courtesy of Svenska Slojdforeningen.)

113

115

114

116

116. Child's coat rack in unfinished pine and birch. By Raimo Simula of Finland. The piece is collapsible. (Courtesy of Norrmark Handicraft.)

117. Suspended baby swing by Ann and Goran Warff of Sweden. (Courtesy of Svenska Slojdforeningen and Boda.)

118. Rope swing in use. By Ann and Goran Warff of Sweden. Forms are made from turned beech. (Courtesy of Svenska Slojdforeningen and Boda.)

119. Rope swing by Ann and Goran Warff of Sweden. (Courtesy of Svenska Slojdforeningen and Boda.)

117

118

119

120. Hanging cradle in beech with canvas.
By Ann and Goran Warff of Sweden.
(Courtesy of Boda.)

121. Swing in turned beech by Ann and
Goran Warff of Sweden. (Courtesy of Boda.)

122. Hanging cradle when collapsed. By Ann
and Goran Warff of Sweden. (Courtesy of
Boda.)

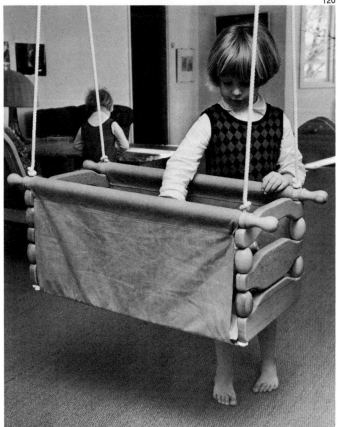

120

121

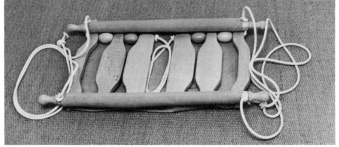

122

123. Rocking form in beech by Ann and Goran Warff of Sweden. (Courtesy of Boda.)

124. Toy forms in birch that stimulate such basic motor movements as twisting, turning, pulling, and pushing. By Pekka Korpijaakko and Jorma Vennola for Aarikka of Finland.

125. Building blocks in unfinished beech. By Kaj Bojesen of Denmark.

126. Postman in painted beech. By Kaj
Bojesen of Denmark.

127. Wooden boat with lacquered surface.
By A/S Riktige Leker of Norway.

128. King's guard in painted beech. By Kaj
Bojesen of Denmark.

129. Monkey in teak, cedar, and ebony. By
Kaj Bojesen of Denmark. Arms and legs are
held in place by rubber bands in the body
core. (Courtesy of the Danish Society of Arts,
Crafts, and Industrial Design.)

130. Elephants in oak. By Kaj Bojesen of
Denmark.

126

127

128

129

130

131. Doll with carriage in painted beech. By Kaj Bojesen of Denmark.

132. Wiener dog by Kaj Bojesen of Denmark.

133. Woodsman with girl and doll in painted beech. By Kaj Bojesen of Denmark.

134. Beech dolls by Kaj Bojesen of Denmark. Rubber bands and pins hold movable parts together.

131

132

133

134

135. Trolls by Arne Tjomsland of Norway. These figures contrast the smooth surface of wood with the fuzz of wool. (Courtesy of the Norsk Design Centrum and Goodwill Productions A/S.)

136. Pet carriage in cane and rush by Kaj Bojesen and R. Wengler of Denmark. (Courtesy of the Danish Society of Arts, Crafts, and Industrial Design.)

137. "Marilyn," smoked oak doll with hemp hair. By Kristian Vedel of Denmark. (Courtesy of Torben Ørskov and the Danish Society of Arts, Crafts, and Industrial Design.)

135

137

136

138

139

138. Birds in smoked and natural oak. By Kristian Vedel of Denmark. (Courtesy of Torben Ørskov and the Danish Society of Arts, Crafts, and Industrial Design.)

139. Unfinished beech vehicles by Kaj Bojesen of Denmark. These forms all come apart and are constructed from blocks which come packed inside the garage. (Courtesy of the Danish Society of Arts, Crafts, and Industrial Design.)

140. Eskimo dolls in teak, oak, and spruce by Arne Tjomsland of Norway. (Courtesy of the Norsk Design Centrum and Goodwill Productions A/S.)

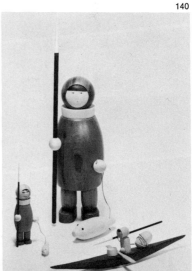

140

141. Pull toy in pine by students of the Finnish School for Woodworking. Center sections are made by gluing two U-shaped forms together.

142. Pine toys made by students of the Finnish School for Woodworking. These forms, along with the forms in Figures 141 and 146, were an experiment in the use of ready-made industrial wood.

143. Beech truck by Kaj Bojesen of Denmark. (Courtesy of the Danish Society of Arts, Crafts, and Industrial Design.)

141

142

143

144. Collapsible, unpainted birch toys by J. O. Nordstrom of Finland. (Courtesy of Luhti Oy.)

145. Sections for collapsible toys in Figure 144.

146. Pine boats by students at the Finnish School for Woodworking.

147. Birch toy (detail of Figure 144.)

145

146

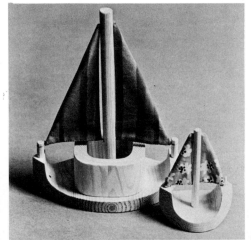

147

148. London bus in painted birch. (Courtesy of Oy Juho Jussila of Finland.)

149. Steamroller in painted birch. (Courtesy of Oy Juho Jussila of Finland.)

150. Old Ford in painted birch by Erkki Jussila of Finland. (Courtesy of Oy Juho Jussila.)

151. Ring figures that come apart, in painted birch. (Courtesy of Brio–K. B. Ilos, Sweden.)

148

149

150

151

152

152. Bent-plywood rocking horse with bent-plywood wagon. By Stig Lonngren, SIR, Sweden. (Courtesy of Svenska Slojdforeningen.)

153. Ferryboat in unfinished birch by Erkki Jussila of Finland. (Courtesy of Oy Juho Jussila.)

154. Skittle car in painted birch by Erkki Jussila of Finland. (Courtesy of Oy Juho Jussila.)

155. "Jumbo," bent plywood with natural finish. Plywood used is ⅜ inch thick. Seat is made of glued felt; wheel rims are wood; treads are rubber. (Courtesy of Brio–K. B. Ilos, Sweden.)

156. "Sitting Bull," bent plywood with natural finish. (Courtesy of Brio–K. B. Ilos, Sweden.)

153

154

155

156

LIGHT FIXTURES

157. Ceiling shade of bentwood pine by Hans-Agne Jakobsson of Sweden. Shade is about 9 inches in diameter and 8 inches high.

158. Pine table lamp with pine splintwood, or veneer, shade. By Hans-Agne Jakobsson of Sweden. Shade uses both straight and bentwood strips and is approximately 8 inches in diameter. The height of the lamp with shade is about 1¼ feet.

159. Ceiling shade in pine by Hans-Agne Jakobsson of Sweden. This form uses bentwood strips for the shade and arc strips for the ribs.

158

159

160. Ceiling shade by Hans-Agne Jakobsson of Sweden, made from dovetailed strips of pine that are 3 millimeters thick. The use of vivid, straight grain is evident on this form.

161. Double ceiling shade of pine veneer bent into tube forms. By Hans-Agne Jakobsson of Sweden.

162. Two pine ceiling shades made from squares and rectangles. By E. V. Luostarinen of Finland.

161

162

163. Pine ceiling shade made from stacked circles, slit and glued. (Courtesy of E. V. Luostarinen of Finland.)

164. Construction of ceiling shade in Figure 162. Individual strips are slit to interlock. They are held tight with glue. (Courtesy of E. V. Luostarinen of Finland.)

165. Gluing technique for shade made with stacked circles. Strips are clamped with clothespins while glue sets. (Courtesy of E. V. Luostarinen of Finland.)

163

164

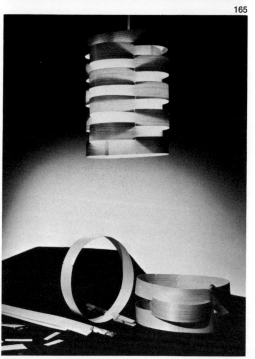

165

166

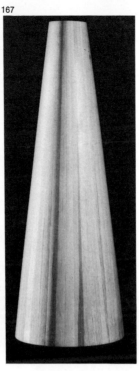

167

166. Ceiling shade in pine made from arc strips, slit and glued as shown. (Courtesy of E. V. Luostarinen of Finland.)

167. Megaphone ceiling shade made from tapered pine strips, glued together. By Jørgen Wolff of Denmark. (Courtesy of the Danish Society of Arts, Crafts, and Industrial Design.)

168. Two ceiling shades in pine by E. V. Luostarinen of Finland. Shade on the left uses vertical bentwood strips, shade on the right has woven strips.

169. Ceiling shade from vertical bentwood strips of pine. By E. V. Luostarinen of Finland. Shade can be used alone or in a series.

170. Ceiling shade made from woven strips of pine. By E. V. Luostarinen of Finland.

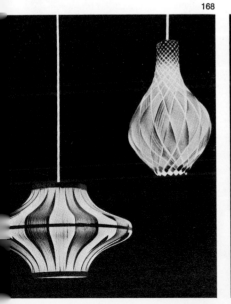

168

169

170

DECORATIVE WOOD FORMS

171. Carved spinning-wheel blades from
nineteenth-century Finland. The spinning
wheel blade was the customary gift from the
bridegroom to his bride. (Courtesy of the
National Museum of Finland.)

171

172

172. Spinning-wheel blade in place on the wheel. (Courtesy of the National Museum of Finland.)

173. Applying the root bands on stave-type buckets and mugs. (Courtesy of the National Museum of Finland.)

174. Stave beer tumbler with roots used as bands. (Courtesy of the National Museum of Finland.)

173

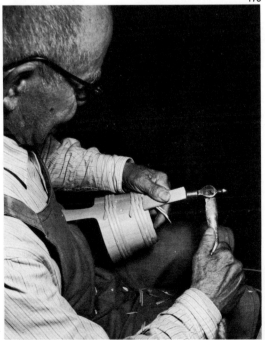

174

175. Root bands (detail). Ends of bands are notched to lock and then tucked under one another. (Courtesy of Konstindustriskolan, Goteborg, Sweden.)

176. Basket made from two bent arcs laced together with root. Handle is made from a bent twig laced with root. (Courtesy of Svenska Slojdforeningen.)

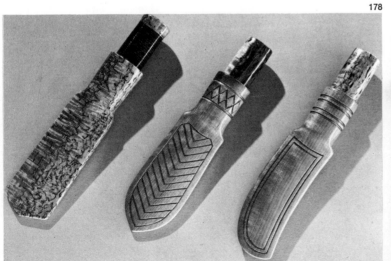

177. Wooden animal forms from teak, oak, and spruce. By Arne Tjomsland of Norway. (Courtesy of the Norsk Design Centrum and Goodwill Productions A/S.)

178. Three knife sheaths formed from glued halves. By Irjo Rosola. (Courtesy of Konstindustriskolan, Goteborg, Sweden.)

179. Traditional Swedish trivet made from interlocking pieces of birch root. The form was originally used by a brewer in a beer keg. (Courtesy of Hemslojdsforbundet for Sverige.)

177

178

179

180. Nutcracker birds made from turned beech. By Ann and Goran Warff of Sweden. (Courtesy of Boda Glassworks.)

181. Wooden puzzle designed for blind and handicapped people. By Gunnar Kanevad of Sweden. (Courtesy of Kollegiet for Sverige-Information.)

182. Horses carved from beech. (Courtesy of Hemslojdsforbundet for Sverige.)

180

181

182

183

183. Salad set in teak by N. Still of Finland. (Courtesy of Norrmark Handicraft.)

184. Spoons by Brigitta Bergh of Finland. (Courtesy of Norrmark Handicraft.)

185. Condiment set in turned teak by Rachel Weyergang of Norway. (Courtesy of the Norsk Design Centrum.)

184   185

186. Knitting balls or string holders in turned teak. By Kaj Bojesen of Denmark. (Courtesy of the Royal Danish Ministry for Foreign Affairs.)

187. Turned salad bowls in teak by Kaj Bojesen of Denmark. The bowls are designed to fit one over the other, with a side opening for the serving set. (Courtesy of the Royal Danish Ministry for Foreign Affairs.)

188. Turned teak bowls by Finn Juhl of Denmark. (Courtesy of Kaj Bojesen and the Royal Danish Ministry for Foreign Affairs.)

189

189. Cutting board with ribs for juice by Nils Koppel of Denmark. (Courtesy of the Danish Society of Arts, Crafts, and Industrial Design.)

190. Three boxes with covers in turned pine, unfinished. These elementary forms reflect great care in the selection and matching of grain figure. Tops were made from four pieces, matched and glued. (Courtesy of the Finnish Design Center.)

191. Cutting boards by Skjøde of Denmark. (Courtesy of the Danish Society of Arts, Crafts, and Industrial Design.)

190

191

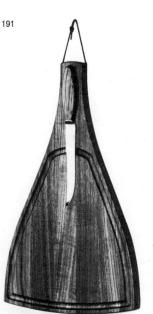

192. Unfinished pine candleholders by Erik Hoglund of Sweden. (Courtesy of Boda and Svenska Slojdforeningen.)

193. Turned candleholders in unfinished pine. By Nanny Still. The selection and matching of grain figure was done with great care. (Courtesy of Norrmark Handicraft, Finland.)

194. Turned candleholder in unfinished pine. By Nanny Still of Finland. (Courtesy of Norrmark Handicraft.)

192

193

194

195. Turned birch candleholders with beads by Kaija Aarikka of Finland. Vegetable dye is used to color forms. Beads are dunked into boiling dye and then buffed on an electric polishing wheel with paraffin wax to fix the color and add gloss to the surface.

196. Candleholders with wooden beads, unfinished, enameled, and stained. By Timo Sarpaneva of Finland. (Courtesy of Aarikka.)

196

197. Chess table in oak, teak, and maple with two drawers. By James Krenov of Sweden.

198. Music stand in pear with two drawers. By James Krenov of Sweden.

199. Music stand in pear (detail). By James Krenov of Sweden.

197

198

199

200

200. Chess table (detail) by James Krenov of Sweden. There is 1/16 inch of space in between the playing squares, and the letters are removable.

201. Tick-tack-toe game in teak by Henning Bang of Denmark. (Courtesy of Den Permanente.)

201

HOLIDAY
WOOD FORMS

202. Christmas wall decoration formed in a manner similar to the St. Thomas cross. (Courtesy of Svenska Slojdforeningen.)

203. St. Thomas cross in balsam by Jorma Karppanen of Finland. Thin slices were carved out of wood and then curled to form the pattern. (Courtesy of A. B. Norna Oy.)

204. Variation on the St. Thomas cross pattern in asp. (Courtesy of Konstindustriskolan, Goteborg, Sweden.)

205. Christmas angel and dove by Salo Skippari of Finland. The angel wings were formed from separate, single pieces, sliced and spread. The wings are notched to keep the slices spread apart. The dove's tail was made from a single piece of wood, sliced and spread. (Courtesy of A. B. Norna Oy.)

206. Christmas tree candle and apple stand from Sweden. (Courtesy of Svenska Slojdforeningen.)

207. Pine Christmas tree candle and apple stand from Sweden. (Courtesy of Svenska Slojdforeningen.)

206

207

208. Hedgehog apple holder by Gunnar
Westman of Denmark. (Courtesy of Peter
Trock and the Danish Society of Arts, Crafts,
and Industrial Design.)

209. Christmas cross from Sweden.
(Courtesy of Svenska Slojdforeningen.)

210. Plate and hot plate by Salo Skippari
of Finland, made from slices of juniper.
The plate is inlaid with juniper.
(Courtesy of A. B. Norna Oy.)

208

209

210

PIPES

211. A craftsman from the Larsen workshop draws the bowl form on the brier block so that the natural surface texture will be preserved at the top of the bowl. (Courtesy of Ole W. O. Larsen of Denmark.)

212. Danish pipe-maker from the Larsen workshop holding up a completed free-form, brier-bowl pipe. This pipe has a one-piece Vulcanite stem and bit. (Courtesy of Ole W. O. Larsen of Denmark.)

213. Three free-form, brier-bowl pipes with natural surfaces preserved at the tops of the bowls. The shanks, or stems on all three pipes were carved from buffalo horn, and the bits, or mouthpieces were fashioned from Vulcanite. (Courtesy of Ole W. O. Larsen of Denmark.)

214. A selection of four free-form, brier-bowl pipes with natural surfaces preserved. The two top pipes use buffalo horn stems and Vulcanite bits. The lower left pipe uses a one-piece Vulcanite stem and bit, and the pipe lower right a bamboo stem and a Vulcanite bit. (Courtesy of Ole W. O. Larsen of Denmark.)

215. Two free-form, brier-bowl pipes with one-piece Vulcanite stems and bits. Vulcanite is a composition material that resists denting and moisture. (Courtesy of Ole W. O. Larsen of Denmark.)

216. Two free-form, brier-bowl pipes with natural surfaces preserved at the bases of the bowls. The pipe craftsman often lets the exotic grain of the brier suggest the form. (Courtesy of Ole W. O. Larsen of Denmark.)

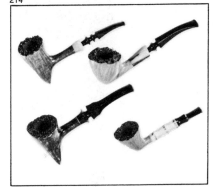

LAPP
WOODCRAFT

217. Details of carving on Lapp magic drum. (Courtesy of Lulea, Sweden, Museum and Pal-Nils Nilsson.)

218. Lapp magic drum (back view) covered with reindeer skin. (Courtesy of Lulea, Sweden, Museum and Pal-Nils Nilsson.)

219. Burl door pulls by Esse Poggats, inlaid with engraved reindeer horn. These were designed for the town hall at Kiruna, Lapland, Sweden. They are a contemporary redefinition of the form used on the Lapp magic drum. (Courtesy of Pal-Nils Nilsson.)

220. Curly birch carry-all with engraved reindeer horn handle. By Esse Poggats. This is another redefinition of the form used on the Lapp magic drum. (Courtesy of Pal-Nils Nilsson.)

221. Lapp salt flask in birch. (Courtesy of Lulea, Sweden, Museum and Pal-Nils Nilsson.)

222. Lapp storage boxes in birch—lower box has reindeer horn inlaid on the cover. (Courtesy of Lulea, Sweden, Museum and Pal-Nils Nilsson.)

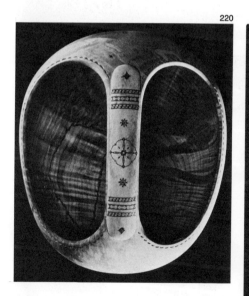

220

221

222

223 Lapp carry-all. (Courtesy of Lulea, Sweden, Museum and Pal-Nils Nilsson.)

224. Lapp covered box in curly birch and inlaid with engraved reindeer horn. By Tore Sunna. (Courtesy of Pal-Nils Nilsson.)

225. Contemporary Lapp birch and burl forms with engraved reindeer horn inlaid on wood surfaces. (Courtesy of Pal-Nils Nilsson.)

223

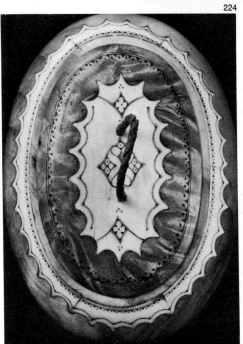

224

225

226

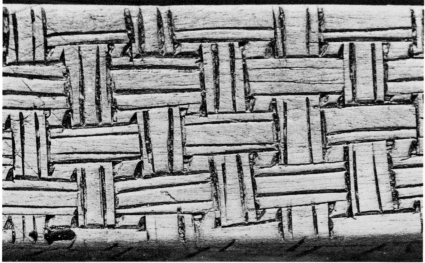

227

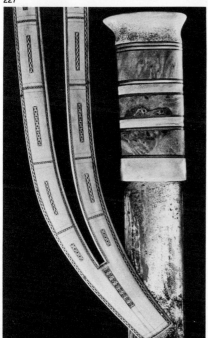

228

226. Lapp carry-all (detail). (Courtesy of Lulea, Sweden, Museum and Pal-Nils Nilsson.)

227. Lapp knife with engraved reindeer-horn sheath. By Sune Enocksson. The handle on this knife has layers of horn, silver, bark, and curly birch. (Courtesy of Pal-Nils Nilsson.)

228. Lapp craftsman rubbing powdered alder bark into horn engravings to contrast the tones of the surface with the cuts. (Courtesy of Pal-Nils Nilsson.)

229. *Kuksa*, Lapp drinking cup (left); and *naappu*, reindeer-milking bowl (right); both by young craftsmen from the studio of Johannes Lauri, Finland. These traditional forms were fashioned from the underground raita burl (a member of the willow family that grows on the Finnish moors). (Courtesy of Maija-Liisa Lauri.)

230. Lapp bowls in beech by Gosta Israelsson of Sweden. (Courtesy of Pal-Nils Nilsson.)

231. Sanding the *kuksa* on a grindstone. (Courtesy of Maija-Liisa Lauri.)

229

230

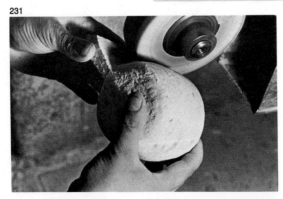

231

233

234

232. Lapp craftsman Esse Poggats begins to remove a birch burl for use in a bowl. The Lapp is attracted to the burl both for its durability and its exotic grain figure. (Courtesy of Pal-Nils Nilsson.)

233. Lapp covered basket plaited from root fiber that has been drawn, washed, and then boiled. (Courtesy of Lulea, Sweden, Museum and Pal-Nils Nilsson.)

234. Contemporary Lapp drinking cup in birch by Sune Enocksson of Sweden. (Courtesy of Pal-Nils Nilsson.)

ACKNOWLEDGMENTS

In addition to the many craftsmen, architects, and manufacturers who contributed to this book, I would like to thank the following organizations and individuals who made my research in Scandinavia possible; Maire Walden and the Finnish Press Bureau; Erkki Savolainen and *Look At Finland* magazine; Sinikka Salokorpi, Juhani Jaskari, and *Avotakka* magazine; the Finnish Design Center and Reino Routamo; the Finnish Society of Crafts and Design and H. O. Gummerus; Ornamo; and Eila Nevenranta, Kaj Franck, Howard Smith, Matti Timola, and Heikki Salminen—all of Finland. Norsk Design Centrum, Alf Bøe, and Janicke Meyer; *Bonytt* magazine; and Dr. and Mrs. Peter Anker—all of Norway. Svenska Slojdforeningen and Birgitta Willen; the Swedish Institute; Anna-Greta Erkner Annerfalk and Kollegiet for Sverige—Information; Claes-Hokan Wihl, his wife, and the staff at Monsanto Scandinavia Ab; *Sweden Now* magazine; Pal-Nils Nilsson; Hemslojdforbundet for Sverige; *Forum* magazine; and the Form Design Center in Malmo—all of Sweden. The Danish Society of Arts, Crafts, and Industrial Design, Bengt Salicath, and Aksel Dahl; Den Permanente and Mrs. Ole Wanscher; the Royal Danish Ministry of Foreign Affairs Press Office; the Danish Minister of Culture; *Mobilia* magazine; the Danish Handicraft School; Ole W. O. Larsen; and John Allpass, Birgit Rastrup-Larsen, Kirsten Dehlholm, Otto Sigvaldi, Ove Hector Nielsen, Mr. and Mrs. Kaj Larsen, and Sandy Willcox—all of Denmark.

For travel arrangements, I would like to thank: the Finnish Travel Association; Finnair; Oy Finnlines Ab; the Finnish Steamship Company; Bore Lines Ab; the Foreign Ministry of Norway; the Norwegian State Railway; Scandinavian Airlines System; the Swedish State Railway; Swedish American Line; the Danish State Railway; the Royal Danish Ministry of Foreign Affairs; and the United Steamship Company of Denmark.

I would like to thank the following photographers and agencies who have work included in this volume: Otso Pietinen; Seppo Saves and Finn 7; Ilmari Kostiainen; Sarja Foto; Valok. M. Hippo; E. Laaksovirta; Studio Wendt; Heikki Savolainen; Heikki Havas; Tima Rima; Kuvakiila; Aulis Nyqvist; Petrelius; Sauren Foto; and Ornamo—all of Finland. Young Thue; *Bonytt* magazine; Foto Design A/S; Arne Svendsen; Rudi Meyer; Norform; Carrebye Foto; and Tiegens Foto—all of Norway. Pal-Nils Nilsson/Tio; Action-bild; Kjell Johansson; Carl Johan De Greer; Sundahl; Studio Granath; Magnus Johnson; Henrik Hultgren; Instituet for Fargfoto; Gert Hogstrom; and Reijo Ruster; all of Sweden. Copenhagen Foto Service; M. Ingemann Sorensen; Mogens Koch; Lundgaard Andersen; Jesper Høm; Jonals Foto; Flemmig Hvidt; Andersen Billeder; Anker Tied-mann; Ellegaard Foto; Rigmor Mydtskov; Steen Rønne; Hammerschmidt Foto; Christopher Hauch; Jørn Freddie; Louis Schnakenburg; E. B. Foto; Steen Jacobsen; Struwing; Bror Bernild; K. Helmer-Petersen; and Jurgen Kriewald—all of Denmark.

MATERIALS FOR FURTHER STUDY

The following books and periodicals may be ordered directly from their publishers in Europe and the United States:

Avotakka (periodical), Hitsaajankatu 10, Helsinki 81, Finland.
Designed in Finland, Et Esplanadikatu 18, Helsinki 13, Finland.
Look at Finland (periodical), Box 10625, Helsinki 10, Finland.
Bonytt (periodical), Bygdoy Alle 9, Oslo 2, Norway.

Forum (periodical), Box 7047, Stockholm 7, Sweden.
Sweden Now (periodical), Warfvinges Vag 26, Stockholm, Sweden.

Dansk Kunsthaandvaerk (periodical), Bredgade 58, 1260 Copenhagen K, Denmark.
Mobilia (periodical), Snekkersten, Denmark.
Møller, Svend Erik, *34 Scandinavian Designers,* Mobilia, Snekkersten, Denmark (1967).

American Scandinavian Review, 127 E. 73 St., New York, N.Y. 10021.
The Architectural Forum, 111 W. 57 St., New York, N.Y.
Craft Horizons, 44 W. 53 St., New York, N.Y. 10019.
Design News, Cahners, 300 E. 42 St., New York, N.Y.

Laliberté, Norman, *Wooden Images,* Van Nostrand Reinhold Co., 450 W. 33 St., New York, N.Y. (1966).
Nutting, Wallace, *Furniture Treasury,* Crowell-Collier Macmillan, New York, N.Y. (1954).
Pye, David, *The Nature of Design,* Van Nostrand Reinhold Co., 450 W. 33 St., New York, N.Y. (1966).
Rottger, *Creative Wood Design,* Van Nostrand Reinhold Co., 450 W. 33 St., New York, N.Y. (1961).
Schutze, *Making Modern Furniture,* Van Nostrand Reinhold Co., 450 W. 33 St., New York, N.Y. (1967).
Simpson, *Fantasy Furniture,* Van Nostrand Reinhold Co., 450 W. 33 St., New York, N.Y. (1968).
Willcox, Donald J., *Wood Design,* Watson-Guptill Publications (1967).

The following Scandinavian schools offer courses in woodcraft:

Ateneum, Railway Square, Helsinki 10, Finland.

Statens Handverks og Kunstindustriskole, Ullevalsvejen 5, Oslo 1, Norway.
Statens Kunstindustriskole, Bergen, Norway.

Konstfackskolan, Valhallavegen 191, Stockholm, Sweden.

Konstindustriskolan, Kristinelundsgatan 6-8, Goteborg C, Sweden.

Kunsthaandvaerkskole, Copenhagen, Denmark.

Scandinavian design and handicraft societies and exhibitions:

The Finnish Design Center, Kasarminkatu 19, Helsinki, Finland.
The Finnish Society of Crafts and Design, Unionkatu 30, Helsinki 10, Finland.
Ornamo, Ainonkatu 3, Helsinki 10, Finland.

Forum, Rosenkrantzgt. 7, Oslo 1, Norway.
Landsforbundet Norsk Brukskunst, Uranienborgvejen 2, Oslo 1, Norway.
Norsk Design Centrum, Drammensvejen 40, Oslo 2, Norway.

The Form Design Center, Malmo, Sweden.
Svenska Slojdforeningen, Nybrogatan 7, Box 7047, Stockholm 7, Sweden.

The Danish Society of Arts, Crafts, and Industrial Design, Bredgade 58, 1260 Copenhagen K, Denmark.
Den Permanente, Vesterport, Copenhagen V, Denmark.